CUSTOMS · COSTUMES AND CULTURES

CELEBRATIONS

by
Jerry Craven

Rourke Publications, Inc.
Vero Beach, Florida 32964

PHOTO CREDITS

Photophile
Picture Library Associates

ACKNOWLEDGEMENTS

I appreciate Ben Smusz and the Gail Fogle family for the photos of the bar and bat mitzvah, as well as Hertner's Camera and Video for helping with those photographs. Thanks to Father Crowe of St. Martin's Church for his help with photographs and information on saints. I'm also grateful to Art Gray for the photo of the christening.

Library of Congress Cataloging-in-Publication Data

Craven, Jerry.
    Celebrations / by Jerry Craven.
        p. cm. — (Customs, costumes, and cultures)
    Includes index.
    Summary: Details the rituals and celebrations that mark special days in a person's life, including birthdays, name days, the bar mitzvah, and marriage.
    ISBN 0-86625-595-8
    1. Holidays—Juvenile literature. 2. Birthdays—Juvenile literature. 3. Special days—Juvenile literature. [1. Birthdays. 2. Holidays.]
I. Title. II. Series.
GT3933.C726 1996
394.2'6—dc20   96-8229
                                                         CIP
                                                         AC

Printed in the U.S.A.

TABLE OF CONTENTS

CHAPTER 1
The Love of Celebrations

People of all cultures enjoy celebrations. They celebrate when something important happens. In most celebrations, people use special symbols to show how they feel.

For example, in Thailand, parents and friends give birds, lizards, or other small animals to children on their birthdays. The children let the animals go free. Freeing animals is a symbol of the freedom of the growing spirit inside all children. It is also a symbol of Buddhism, the official religion of Thailand. Buddhists believe that people should not injure or cage animals.

What's the difference between a festival and a celebration? A festival is a special day that happens at the same time each year. Thanksgiving, Ramadan, and Hanukkah are all festivals. Celebrations, however, can come at any time. They are for special events such as weddings and important birthdays.

During birthday celebrations, children in Latino communities often hit a piñata as part of the fun. Candy inside the piñata scatters when someone breaks it.

A Malay-style wedding celebration can last an entire day. The bride and groom wear special costumes. They celebrate with friends and relatives for many hours.

Just like festivals, celebrations can be times for fancy costumes and fun traditions. When else besides on a birthday is it fun to give or get a spanking? Also, only on her wedding day would a woman wear a white gown with a train so long that she needs help walking with it.

People have celebrations for days important in their own lives and the lives of their families and friends.

CHAPTER 2
Reading the Future on the First Birthday

Whether they live in China or America, many Chinese people believe that the first year of life is the most dangerous. So on a child's first birthday, parents and friends bring many symbols of good luck. For Chinese, red is a lucky color, so many of the gifts they bring are red. Eggs dyed red are especially good gifts. Because eggs are symbols of life, red eggs stand for a lucky life. Also, families serve noodles as part of the birthday meal. Long noodles stand for long life—the longer the noodles, the luckier the child.

Fortune-telling is a part of the child's first birthday. The family puts the one-year-old on the floor next to some special things such as an **abacus** (A buh kus), a writing pen, a coin and a piece of cloth. Then they watch to see what the child picks up.

The first thing the child touches is a key to the future. If it is the pen, the child will be a writer. The cloth means the child might work as a tailor, making clothes. The coin means the child will be rich.

According to tradition, a Chinese child will have only one birthday party. This takes place on the first birthday. The person must live another sixty years before having another birthday party.

This Chinese mother is carrying her one-year-old to a party. Many believe the child will give clues to the future by picking out a gift.

If they follow the old traditions, Chinese people don't celebrate another birthday until they are sixty-one years old. At age sixty-one a person becomes a wise elder. At the birthday celebration, family and friends read aloud the person's fortune from the first birthday party. Part of the fun is to see if the person became what the fortune telling had predicted.

This Chinese woman is celebrating her sixty-first birthday. The red dye on her mouth comes from chewing a special leaf. Among many Chinese, red is a color of good luck.

7

CHAPTER 3
Where Did Birthday Candles Come From?

A cake doesn't mean anything special until someone puts candles on it. Then everyone knows the cake is for a birthday.

As traditions go, putting candles on a birthday cake is not an old idea. The custom began in Germany about 200 years ago. People thought birthdays were dangerous times for a child. They used the candles to keep bad luck away.

For centuries, people used candles in religious ceremonies. They made the candles from beeswax, which was rare and expensive. People believed angels liked the special light of candles. They began to use birthday candles so angels would be close to children on their birthdays.

At first, people put only tiny candles on a cake, one candle for each year plus an extra one "to grow on." Blowing out the candles was a way for children to feel in control of their lives.

Candle makers in Germany began making more and more fancy candles. One favorite was a **twelve-year candle.** This was a tall, thick piece of wax made with many colors and decorations.

For people the world over, a birthday celebration wouldn't be complete without a cake and candles.

Sometimes people use one candle for each ten years. How old is Grandpa on this birthday?

The candle had twelve marks on it from the bottom to the top. On a child's first birthday, the family bought a twelve-year candle, lit it, and let it burn down to the first mark. Then they put the candle away for the next year. On the child's twelfth birthday, they burned the candle all the way down to nothing.

Today, most birthday candles are tiny and do not burn for long. They are made for being lighted only once. People buy the candles only for one reason: to serve as a symbol for a birthday.

CHAPTER 4
The Christening Celebration: Protecting the Child

Before Christianity came to Europe, people asked different gods to protect their children. Just after a baby was born, they had a celebration to give the baby its own special god to watch over it. This was called the baby's **godparent** (GAHD payr unt).

When the people of Europe became Christian, they changed the celebration. Instead of naming a god in the celebration, they named a real person. Today, people still use the words "godfather" and "godmother."

The celebration was called a christening, and it was performed in a church. Parents worried that they might die before the baby was grown. If that happened, who would take care of their child? The idea was that the godparents would take over. For boys, parents chose two godfathers and one godmother. For girls, they chose two godmothers and one godfather.

Today, many people still ask friends and family members to be godparents to their new babies. Many godparents take their job seriously. They visit the child and offer special help and advice all through the child's life.

This family is christening a child in a Roman Catholic ceremony.

CHAPTER 5
Special Birthdays for Japanese Children

In the past, before people knew what caused disease, many children died before they could grow into adults. Japanese people believed that the most dangerous ages for children were three, five, and seven. They made up special traditions to help children survive these times of danger.

One important tradition became a national birthday celebration. They called it *shichi-go-san* (see chee goh san), which means *seven-five-three*. On shichi-go-san day, all children who turn seven, five, or three during that year take part in a ceremony. Parents dress their children in costumes and take them to a nearby temple. The girls wear colorful **kimonos** (kuh MOH nohz) tied with a wide sash. The boys wear suits. All the children carry decorated paper bags.

These Japanese twins and their family are celebrating their fifth birthday on shichi-go-san day in Tokyo.

This birthday girl is about to go into a temple in Tokyo with her older sister.

For her third birthday party on shichi-go-san day, this girl wears a special dress called a kimono.

At the temple, priests give the children blessings. Near the temples, people sell good luck charms, toys, and special candies. Parents buy these treats to put into the children's bags.

Today parents do not worry as much about their children dying as people did in the past. Now, shichi-go-san is a kind of fancy birthday party where everyone honors children. Many Japanese who live in America keep following the customs of shichi-go-san.

CHAPTER 6
The Name Day Celebration

In some parts of the world, families have a special celebration called *name day*. It is a day to honor a special family member. The celebration is like a birthday party. In fact, sometimes the name day party takes the place of a birthday party. However, name day almost never falls on the person's birthday.

Most families who celebrate name day go to the Roman Catholic church. Many Roman Catholic families name their children after a saint. The custom of naming a child after a saint came from an old belief that the saint would treat the child as special. Families celebrate name day on the saint's day. A saint's day is the day on which the saint died.

Many Roman Catholics name their sons for saints like this one. This is Saint Martin de Porres, who died in 1639.

A popular saint among Vietnamese Americans is Saint Andrew Phu Yen, who died in the year 1644.

SAINT ANDREW PHU YEN
CATECHIST
PROTO-MARTYR OF VIETNAM

1625 BORN IN PHU YEN VIETNAM

1644 MARTYRED BY ORDER OF THE
KING IN QUANG NAM VIETNAM

SKULL IS KEPT IN IESUITCURIA IN ROME ITALY

BODY KEPT IN CATHEDRAL OF MACAO
PRESENTLY IN ST FRANCIS XAVIER CHURCH (CHINA)

SAINT ANDREW PLEASE PRAY FOR US

Native Americans of the San Blas Islands off the coast of Central America have an unusual way to name their children. They do not give a child a name until the child is one year old. They believe the child isn't a full human being until it has lived for a year in this world.

Among some people in Ethiopia, parents give their children false names when they are born. Then, when children are one year old, parents give the real names. Giving a false name, they believe, is a way to trick evil spirits who might harm or kill a baby.

CHAPTER 7
The Dream-Quest and the Girl's Dance

Native Americans didn't always celebrate birthdays. However, they did keep track of how old their children were. Among many tribes, the mother counted each winter by carving a notch for her child on a piece of wood. Native Americans often called years *snows.* Counting the notches would give the number of snows, or years, the child had lived.

For some tribes of Native Americans, there are special ceremonies for a boy before he goes on his dream-quest.

At age thirteen, a Native American girl might celebrate becoming an adult with a girl's dance ceremony.

At about age twelve, a boy left his home and stayed for a time in the wilderness. He went to have a dream that would tell him something important about himself and his future. Often the boy ate no food for a long time while he waited for a dream. He hoped a wise spirit would come and give him advice. Most boys thought the dream spirit would be in the shape of an animal.

In many tribes, Native Americans held a "girl's dance" celebration for girls turning thirteen. Friends and family danced and threw money to the girls to keep them dancing. At the end of the ceremony, the family poured water over the girl's head. This act stood for the washing away of childhood.

Both the dream-quest and the girl's dance were ceremonies to celebrate leaving childhood and becoming an adult.

CHAPTER 8
The Bar Mitzvah Celebration

An important celebration for Jewish boys comes at age thirteen. In a special ceremony, he becomes a *bar mitzvah,* which means *son of the commandments.* The thirteenth birthday celebration is also called a bar mitzvah. On that day, the boy takes on the religious duties of a man.

It takes years to prepare for a proper bar mitzvah. A boy must study the laws of the Jewish religion. He must learn prayers in Hebrew because he will say them aloud in a **synagogue** (SI nuh gahg) as part of his bar mitzvah. Along with the prayers, the boy reads from holy writing. He also gives thanks to his parents and other people who taught him about his religion.

As part of his bar mitzvah celebration, this boy is receiving the blessings of a rabbi.

Sometimes a bar mitzvah celebration is held for more than one boy. These two boys are holding copies of the Torah, an important book in the Jewish religion.

For most boys, there is a grand birthday party after the ceremony. Friends and family members give him gifts as on his earlier birthdays. Bar mitzvah gifts are different, though. After the bar mitzvah, the boy is looked upon as a man in many ways. No one gives toys for a bar mitzvah birthday. Toys are for children. Instead, the boy gets gifts adults use in the Hebrew community, such as special clothing worn for leading prayers.

After the bar mitzvah, a boy joins other men in leading religious celebrations, for he has become an adult in matters of religion.

CHAPTER 9
Celebrating Bat Mitzvah

In Hebrew tradition, women didn't have the same religious duties as men. Men led prayers, planned festivals, and performed most other ceremonies. However, today some Jewish people think men and women should have equal roles in religion. Many Jewish groups have welcomed women as **rabbis** (RA biiz), or religious leaders.

One new addition to Jewish ceremonies has been the *bat mitzvah*. This is a celebration for girls that is like the bar mitzvah for boys.

The bat mitzvah is a new celebration that welcomes girls into the Jewish religious community, just as boys are welcomed with the bar mitzvah.

As part of her bat mitzvah celebration, this girl is reading a prayer.

On her thirteenth birthday, a girl becomes a *daughter of the commandments,* or a bat mitzvah. This is an important ceremony that welcomes her into adulthood. After that, in the religious community, she is no longer a girl, but a woman. As with a boy's bar mitzvah, the family gives the bat mitzvah girl a special kind of birthday party. Because bat mitzvah is a coming-of-age ceremony, the girl's family and friends give her birthday gifts for an adult.

A PARENT'S PRAYER

The parents of the children being honored at bar mitzvah and bat mitzvah celebrations say this prayer: "Blessed is God who has now freed me from bearing full responsibility for this person."

CHAPTER 10
The Birthday Spanking

One odd way many Americans celebrate people's birthdays is by spanking them. No one knows for sure where the custom came from. A good guess is that the birthday spanking is supposed to be like the person's first spanking. A midwife or a doctor used to spank a baby when it was born to help the baby begin breathing.

Another guess has to do with an ancient ceremony used to get rid of evil spirits. People once believed that bad spirits could get into someone's body and cause trouble. Evil spirits did not like pain. A good way to make spirits leave people was to spank them. Rather than stay and feel pain, the evil spirits would go away.

Long ago, people also believed children were more open to evil spirits on some days than others. A birthday was one of the dangerous days. A child's birthday must have seemed a good time to get rid of all the evil spirits that got into the child during the year.

Today, people give birthday spankings only because it is a custom. No one gives a hard spanking. It is done for fun. The birthday child gets one swat for each year, plus one to grow on. Some jokers give several more swats, each for a reason such as "to get rich on," "to go to school on," or "to be happy on."

On their birthdays, girls and boys should be ready for a birthday spanking. It is as much a part of birthday celebrations as the traditional cake and candles.

CHAPTER 11
The Special Quinciñera Celebration

Many Latino people in the United States and Mexico celebrate an important day for girls. This is a girl's fifteenth birthday. The celebration is called a *quinciñera* (keen see NYER uh), taken from the Spanish word that means *fifteen.* Some families plan the quinciñera many months or even years in advance.

A quinciñera celebration is a day-long event. Often the day begins with the family going to a special morning church service. Usually the family invites many people to lunch. At night comes the big party.

Women often wear long, colorful dresses. The designs can be traced back to Spain. The men wear black pants and white shirts. Many families ask a *mariachi* (mahr ee AH chee) band to play traditional music, and people dance. Band members wear traditional costumes of black and white, often with red trimmings. They play guitar, bass, brass horns, and violins.

The special person at a quinciñera is, of course, the birthday girl. People pay much attention to her, especially the young men. The celebration is a kind of coming-out party, a public statement that the girl is now a woman.

THE FIRST DATE

In many Latino families, young men may not date a young woman until after her quinciñera.

An important part of many quinciñera celebrations is traditional Mexican dancing.

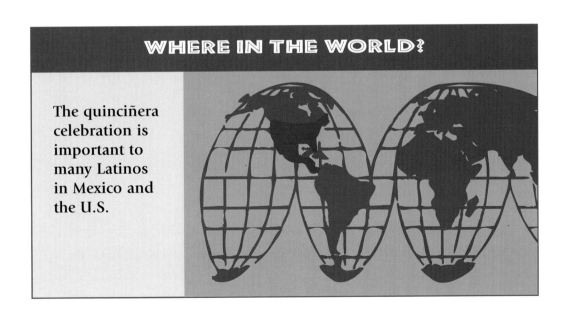

WHERE IN THE WORLD?

The quinciñera celebration is important to many Latinos in Mexico and the U.S.

CHAPTER 12
The Ceremony of the House Key

An important celebration in the United States and several other countries comes when a young person turns twenty-one. In the past, the twenty-first birthdays were more important for men than for women. People called the birthday party a "key party."

In some cultures, it is the custom for a father to give his son a key to the house on the son's twenty-first birthday.

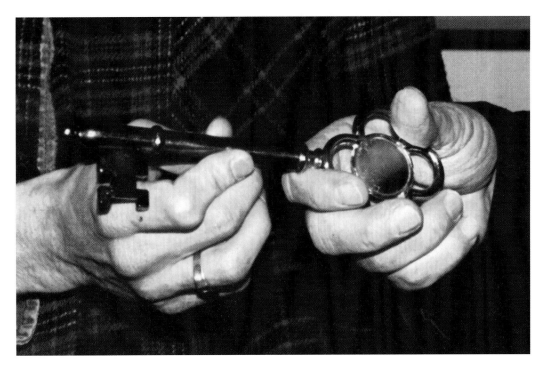

These days, the "key to the house" isn't a key to a lock. It is a symbol in the shape of a large key.

In the time before cars, young people had less freedom to come and go as they wished. Fathers and mothers demanded to know where their older children were going before giving their permission. When young men turned twenty-one, they officially became adults. At the key party, the parents gave their son a key to their house. This was a way of saying, "You are now old enough to come and go without our permission."

Today, not many people give real keys at key parties. However, the custom of key parties is still alive, perhaps more in England and other countries than in the United States. At key parties, parents still give a key, but the key is a symbol. It isn't a real key. It might be a huge brass key or a large wooden key painted silver or gold, or covered in bright silver-colored foil.

Even without a key party, many people in the United States believe the twenty-first birthday is important enough for a big celebration.

CHAPTER 13
Celebrating Marriage

Marriage is an important celebration around the world. In the United States, there are many kinds of marriage ceremonies. Some couples choose strange places for getting married. For example, some couples have gotten married while skydiving. Some have married on baseball fields. Some have even married underwater while wearing **scuba** (SKOO buh) gear.

In the most popular kind of wedding ceremony, the bride wears a fancy white dress and the groom wears a tuxedo. Often many bridesmaids and groomsmen take part in the wedding. Sometimes hundreds of people attend the wedding.

Most American couples celebrate marriage with a ceremony in which the bride wears a beautiful white dress and the groom wears a black tuxedo.

This American couple is celebrating their wedding in the traditions their parents brought from Thailand and Laos.

Traditional weddings take much planning, time, and money. There are businesses that make the ceremony easier by doing all the planning. To save money, some brides rent dresses rather than buy them. Grooms and groomsmen usually rent their tuxedos. Many people work for days to make the ceremony beautiful and romantic.

Some couples choose more simple ceremonies. They get married in a small church or in the home of a friend or family member. Others choose to have the ceremony in a beautiful outdoor setting. One thing all wedding ceremonies have in common is that the couple says to everyone that they choose to be husband and wife.

CHAPTER 14
Celebrations Throughout Life

People celebrate special events from birth to death, and the celebrations take many forms. Some are fun and playful. Others are serious. Celebrations can be times for great joy or times for grief.

All cultures have celebrations for children as they grow up. The dream-quest and the girl's dance are examples of coming-of-age celebrations among Native Americans. Among people in the Latino culture, the quinciñera is an important celebration of a girl becoming a woman. Jewish communities like to celebrate children's thirteenth birthdays with bar and bat mitzvah parties.

As adults, people celebrate graduations, marriages, and anniversaries. Young couples begin the cycle of celebrations all over again when they have children and honor them with name days, special birthdays, and so on.

A final celebration held in honor of a person's life is a funeral. People think of a celebration as being fun and happy, so many do not think of a funeral as a celebration. However, many believe a funeral is both a serious time of grief and a time to celebrate life.

Many people think of a dance when they hear the word "celebration." This couple from Nepal is dancing as part of their engagement celebration.

GLOSSARY

abacus (A buh kus) – a tool for adding and subtracting, made up of moveable beads set within a frame.

godparents (GAHD payr unts) – a man and a woman named in a christening ceremony to have a special relationship with the child being christened.

kimono (kuh MOH noh) – a dress worn by Japanese girls and women for special events.

mariachi (mahr ee AH chee) – a type of Latino music often played for special celebrations. The band that plays the music is also called *mariachi*.

quinciñera (keen see NYER uh) – in the United States and Mexico, a celebration of a Latino girl's fifteenth birthday.

rabbi (RA bii) – a religious leader within the Jewish community.

scuba (SKOO buh) – a device that allows divers to breathe while underwater. The letters stand for **s**elf **c**ontained **u**nderwater **b**reathing **a**pparatus.

shichi-go-san (see chee goh san) – a national birthday celebration in Japan for children who have turned seven, five, or three during the year. *Shichi-go-san* means *seven-five-three* in Japanese.

synagogue (SI nuh gahg) – a house of worship for Jewish people.

twelve-year candle (TWELV yeer KAN dul) – a special candle popular in Germany that was used each birthday for the first twelve years of a child's life.

INDEX